D

THE
MOHAWK
INDIANS

THE JUNIOR LIBRARY OF
AMERICAN INDIANS

THE MOHAWK INDIANS

Janet Hubbard-Brown

CHELSEA HOUSE PUBLISHERS
New York Philadelphia

FRONTISPIECE The Mohawk chief Joseph Brant.

CHAPTER TITLE ORNAMENT A depiction of a tattoo representing
the Turtle Clan; taken from an 18th-century French illustration.

Chelsea House Publishers

EDITORIAL DIRECTOR Richard Rennert
EXECUTIVE MANAGING EDITOR Karyn Gullen Browne
EXECUTIVE EDITOR Sean Dolan
COPY CHIEF Robin James
PICTURE EDITOR Adrian G. Allen
ART DIRECTOR Robert Mitchell
MANUFACTURING DIRECTOR Gerald Levine
SYSTEMS MANAGER Lindsey Ottman
PRODUCTION COORDINATOR Marie Claire Cebrián-Ume

The Junior Library of American Indians
SENIOR EDITOR Sean Dolan

Staff for THE MOHAWK INDIANS
COPY EDITOR Danielle Janusz
EDITORIAL ASSISTANTS Nicole Greenblatt, Joy Sanchez
ASSISTANT DESIGNER John Infantino
PICTURE RESEARCHER Lisa Kirchner
COVER ILLUSTRATOR Vilma Ortiz

Printed and bound in the United States of America.

3 5 7 9 8 6 4

Library of Congress Cataloging-in-Publication Data
Hubbard-Brown, Janet.
The Mohawk Indians/by Janet Hubbard-Brown.
  p. cm.—(The Junior Library of American Indians)
Includes bibliographical references and index.
Summary: Examines the history, culture, and daily life of the Mohawk
Indians.
  ISBN 0-7910-1667-6
  ISBN 0-7910-1991-8 (pbk.)
1. Mohawk Indians—Juvenile literature. [1. Mohawk Indians. 2. Indians
of North America.] I. Title. II. Series.   93-18247
E99.M8H82 1993   CIP
973'.04975—dc20   AC

CONTENTS

CHAPTER **1**

The Fall from Sky World

Long, long ago, according to the Mohawks, there was another world called Sky World. Life there was similar to life in this world. A very special tree grew in the center of Sky World. It bore all kinds of fruit, and no one was supposed to disturb that tree in any way. One man was given the job of protecting that tree, which was called the Tree of Life.

Then that man got married, and when his wife became pregnant she started craving strange foods. Though her husband gave her the foods she wanted, the woman soon grew curious about the tree with its different fruits. She decided she wanted some of the bark, roots, and fruit from the Tree of Life, but her husband refused to let her take any.

Then the woman began to dream about a place that supposedly existed beneath the tree. She thought about this place all the time. She asked her husband what he knew about it, but he said that he knew nothing about it because it was forbidden to dig around the tree. This only made the woman more determined than ever to know, and she finally convinced her husband to dig around the tree's roots. Beneath the tree was a huge hole.

The woman leaned over and peered into the hole, but she was unable to see anything. She leaned further over the edge of the hole, and then she started to fall. As she toppled through the hole, she managed to grab a strawberry plant with one hand and tobacco leaves with the other.

All the woman could hear as she fell was the whooshing sound of a bird rattle. All she could see below her was water, but a flock of birds flew up to see what this falling object was, and they caught her and carried her down to the water. The birds asked a giant sea turtle if they could put the woman on his back, and the turtle agreed. The animals asked the woman who she was and where she was from. The woman, who already missed her home, explained to them that her world was land, but this world was all water. The animals explained to the homesick woman that there was more land beneath the water, and they took turns diving to bring some earth up to the woman.

They all failed, until finally the otter volunteered. The otter stayed under the water for such a long time that as he came back to the surface he died, but he was holding a little piece of earth in his paw.

The animals placed the earth on the sea turtle's back, and the earth and the turtle both began to grow. In order to keep the land growing, the woman walked in a circle, following the sun. The land grew and began to take shape as the world.

In a short time, the woman gave birth to a baby girl, and when that girl became a woman she gave birth to twin sons. One twin was born normally, but the other broke through his mother's side, killing her. The grandmother was left to raise the twins. She named the twin who had been born out of his mother's side Teharonhiawako, which means Holder of the Heavens, and the other she called Sawiskera, or Mischievous One. Because she blamed *Teharonhiawako* for causing her daughter's death, she was very unkind to him.

The twins fought over everything; they had even fought while in the womb waiting to be born. When the twins became men, the grandmother died, and the two young men fought over the body. Her favorite grandson, Sawiskera, wanted to kick her body off the edge of the world, but Teharonhiawako wanted to bury her in the earth because she felt so much a part of it. Sawiskera pulled off the Grandmother's head and threw it into the air, where it became the moon, which lights up the night world.

Teharonhiawako then began creating various animals and flowers, but Sawiskera would try to change whatever his brother created. Teharonhiawako made the rose, and his brother put thorns on it. Teharonhiawako created gentle animals like the moose and the deer, and Sawiskera caused the mountain lion to want to kill them. After this went on for some time, they decided to compete in games until one became the victor. Teharonhiawako won, and the two brothers decided to divide the world in half. Night would belong to Sawiskera and day to Teharonhiawako.

Now Teharonhiawako wanted to create a being in his likeness from the natural world. He decided to create more than one being, giving to each the same instructions, and over time he would watch to see who obeyed them. He made the first being from the bark of a tree, the second from the foam of the ocean, the third from the black soil, and the last from the red earth. The human forms he created took their colors from the elements out of which they were created—yellow, white, black, and red.

Teharonhiawako gave life to each of the forms. The white being was the most curious, and after the black and yellow humans began to slowly move about, a fight soon broke out among the three. Teharonhiawako noticed that the fourth was still sitting peacefully on the ground, and he knew in that instant that the four beings he had created could not live together in the same place. He explained to them that in order to learn to get along, they would first have to be separated. He told them they would be reunited when he sent a messenger to visit each of them. The messenger would also show them a way to be thankful for all the good things of the earth and a way to respect other living creatures.

Teharonhiawako took the white, the black, and the yellow beings across the ocean and placed them far away from each other. The red being he kept in his place of origin, where he lived in harmony with the natural world.

He was called Onkwehonwe, which means Original Being. Teharonhiawako was very pleased. He thought that all the beings would have a chance to learn the reason for their existence. They would also learn a good way to live.

This creation story has been told many times among the Mohawks, or *Kanienkehaka* (ga-nyen-ge-HA-ga), as they call themselves in their own language. It is one of many stories that helps to keep the Mohawk culture alive, and it tells us much about how they view the world.

The Mohawks are one of the five Iroquois nations. The others are the Oneidas, the Onondagas, the Cayugas, and the Senecas. The Iroquois tribes lived in central New York, west of the Hudson River. The Mohawks were the easternmost Iroquois tribe, and the Senecas were the westernmost. The Cayugas lived nearer the Senecas, the Oneidas nearer the Mohawks, and the Onondagas in the middle. Though they lived separately, the Iroquois nations shared similar languages and ways of life.

For hundreds of years, the Mohawks lived in the Mohawk River valley, near what is today the city of Albany, New York. Hunters and gatherers at first, the Mohawks soon also became traders and farmers. Their country was mountainous, heavily wooded, and filled with wildlife, and for many years the Mohawks were a powerful nation that decided the fortunes of many peoples—Indian and non-Indian alike. In the 1300s or 1400s, they formed the Iroquois Confederacy with their neighboring nations for the purpose of keeping peace among themselves. (A *confederacy* is a union of tribes or nations that functions as one unit.) The English settlers who began to arrive in Iroquois territory in the 1600s called the tribes of the confederacy the *Five Nations*. The Five Nations used diplomacy, commerce, and warfare to combat the settlers who overran their homelands, but by the end of the 1700s the Mohawks could resist no longer, and their nation was divided forever.

Today, the Mohawks live in eastern New York State and the province of Ontario in Canada. Though many non-Indians who came into contact with them over the years remarked on their kindness and humanity, they also became known for their fierceness as warriors, and much of their history since the arrival of white settlers has consisted of their struggle to hold on to their land and traditions. But before that, the Mohawk knew a more secure existence as the Kanien-kehaka, the People of the Place of Flint. ▲

Mohawk women prepare food. Mohawk women played a central role in Mohawk society and were referred to as the "mothers of the nation."

CHAPTER 2

The People of the Place of Flint

The history of the Mohawks in the northeastern part of the United States has been traced back more than 3,000 years. Their ancient ancestors were hunters and gatherers who moved often in order to follow their animal prey. They probably migrated to northeastern New York between 1700 B.C. and 1200 B.C. Around 1000 B.C. they began developing a central base area where they lived between hunting and fishing trips, and they traded with people from all over the continent. Among some of the items found at the sites once inhabited by these ancient Indians of what came to be known as the Early Woodland Period of the Indian peoples of the Northeast are conch shells from the Gulf of Mexico, copper from Lake Superior, silver from Ontario, and Canadian grizzly-bear teeth from the Rocky Mountains.

The Middle Woodland Period began around A.D. 200. The peoples began to build larger, more permanent villages near rivers. Individual houses were made from earth and wood and were big enough for several families to live in. As travel through the dense woods of their homeland was often difficult and dangerous, the Indians relied on canoes for transportation along the many rivers and lakes of the region. They continued to hunt game and gather wild plants, but they also began to cultivate their own sources of food, mainly by growing corn. The original Native American corn planters were the people of Central America; the Indians of the Northeast probably learned about corn through trade contacts with Native American people farther west.

More changes occurred in the Late Woodland Period, which lasted from A.D. 1000 to 1300. The Indian peoples now tended to build their villages on hilltops rather than rivers, probably because hilltop locations were easier to defend from attack. Most hilltop villages were surrounded by *palisades*—walls of long poles built for defense. At some settlements, ditches were dug outside the palisades for additional protection, and barricades were erected inside the walls. Obviously, warfare was not unknown to the Late Woodlands peoples.

The Iroquoian tradition began around A.D. 1300. The Iroquois were several different groups of people, separated geographically, who spoke similar languages and had social customs and religious beliefs in common. Their homes, called *longhouses*, were large, rectangular structures with doors at each end. They were made of wooden poles covered with elm bark. Inside was a central row of hearths for cooking and heating. As many as 10 families lived together, sharing the hearths but maintaining separate living areas. The Iroquois built stronger palisades than their ancestors had, which suggests that warfare had intensified. Constant fighting seems also to have interfered with the operation of the intercontinental trade network that had linked the various Native American peoples for so long.

This is also the period when the Kanienkehaka, or the Mohawks, formed their own nation. Kanienkehaka means "People of the Place of Flint." Flint is a hard kind of stone used by the Mohawks and other Indians to start fires and as arrowheads.

The Mohawks lived in three large villages located on the south side of the Mohawk

River, near what is now the city of Albany in New York state. Villages were located on hilltops close to the lakes and rivers that provided the major routes of travel. Small villages contained about 30 longhouses, but larger ones held as many as 100. A typical house contained a central row of four to five hearths. Two families usually shared a hearth. Platforms built along the inner walls were used for seating during the day and sleeping at night.

Women were highly valued members of Mohawk society. Because they were the givers of life, they were often referred to as the "mothers of the nation," and the Mohawks believed that long ago a female god had given corn, beans, and squash to the people. Because women performed the farm work, they were considered the owners of their families' fields, and they were also in charge of the distribution of food. When a man and a woman married, food was exchanged between their families as a symbol of the mutual cooperation that a married couple and the entire community needed in order to prosper.

Each person in the community was considered a member of his or her mother's clan. Mohawk clans were named after animals— the Bear, the Wolf, and the Turtle. Two people of the same clan could not marry each other. A typical household was headed by an elder woman and included her daughters and the younger women's husbands and children. Sons lived with their mothers until they married.

The Mohawk nation was divided into two sections, or *moieties*. A moiety is a grouping of clans. The Wolf and Turtle clans made up one moiety, and the Bear clan formed the other.

Besides farming, Mohawk women gathered fruits, nuts, and wild potatoes. In the early spring, they collected sap from maple trees, which they used to sweeten tea and dishes made from corn. Sometimes men and women from all three clans organized deer hunts, during which they could catch and kill as many as 100 animals.

Mohawk men provided food for the community by hunting elk, deer, moose, bear, beaver, partridge, and wild turkey. They used bows and arrows for hunting, wooden traps to capture deer, and spears and nets to catch birds and fish.

Mohawk life was not all work and no play. The Mohawks especially liked to play a game that today is known as lacrosse. Another pastime, called snow snakes, was popular in winter. A snow snake was a long pole made of polished hickory wood. It measured about one inch at the top, gradually narrowing to one-half inch at the bottom, and was about five to seven feet long. The snow snake was thrown so that it slid along packed snow. The object of the game was to make the snow snake travel the farthest distance.

Mohawk life was filled with ceremonies and rituals. There were three basic themes common to all the rituals: renewal of life and health, giving thanks to the natural and supernatural or spirit worlds, and death rites that recognized the ties between the living and the dead. Many of the ceremonies were organized around a yearly cycle of activities, based on the phases of the moon. *Midwinter* was considered the turning point of the year. It occurred five nights following the appearance of a new moon after the winter solstice, which usually falls on or around December 22.

Midwinter marked the end of one year and the beginning of the next. It lasted nine days.

Iroquois men playing a game of snow snakes. This drawing was done by a Seneca man, Jesse Cornplanter, in 1903.

Game of snowsnake

Copyright-Frederick Starr-1903.

Certain rites and rituals were performed each day. On the first day, a pure-white dog was strangled and then burned. The smoke from the burning carcass was thought to carry people's messages to the spirits. Then messengers, called the Uncles, went through each house in a Mohawk village to announce the start of midwinter. While inside, a messenger took a large wooden paddle and stirred the ashes in every hearth. This rite represented the renewal of the community and the awakening of life forces for the coming year.

The Mohawks believed in a religion that saw life forces in many forms. These animals, objects, or forces had a certain power called *orenda* (o-REN-da). Because life forces could affect humans, people had to treat everything with care and respect. Certain people in the community had special abilities to use these powers to help others, while others—witches—had powers that could be used to harm others. Witches might put dangerous potions into someone's food or drink, or transform themselves into animals so they could wander near their victims without arousing suspicion.

Dreams were extremely important to the Mohawks, who believed that they expressed a person's innermost thoughts and desires. The Mohawks believed that illness could occur if the desires in one's dreams were not realized and expressed. Everyone in the community was expected to help a dreamer fulfill his or her wish. For example, if a person dreamed about visiting someone, then it would be important to make that happen. If a dream was difficult to understand, the dreamer consulted people who had special powers to discover a dream's hidden meaning. The dreams of the Mohawk bound the people together.

During midwinter, several days were spent interpreting and fulfilling people's dreams. Dreamers would go from house to house asking others to guess their dreams. They gave hints or told riddles about things that had appeared in a particular dream. The guesser would give to the dreamer an object that she or he believed was seen in the dream. When someone offered the correct object, the dreamer kept it and returned all others to their owners. The dream-guessing was a kind of storytelling that provided the Mohawks with entertainment during the long, cold winters in their homeland.

White and purple beads called wampum played an important part in Mohawk society. Wampum was made from clam shells that came from present-day Long Island and New Jersey. The shells were cut into pieces and made into small beads that were strung together and made into belts. Different patterns gave different messages. The pictures in the belt helped people remember important agreements or events in history. Wampum was used at many special events. The story of a special event was "talked into the wampum" and thereby preserved forever.

The Mohawks liked to tell a story that illustrated the symbolic importance of wampum in their culture. Once, the Mohawks captured a young man of the Wampanoag nation, with whom they were at war. He was carefully guarded so that he would not escape. One day, a Mohawk hunter came running into the village with the news that he had seen a bird covered with wampum beads. A band of hunters rushed out to try to capture this wonderful bird. None of them was successful. Finally, the young captive asked if he could try. The chief gave his permission, though the warriors were angry that he said yes. The boy's arrow pierced the bird's heart on the first try. The boy married the chief's daughter, and with the marriage came peace between the two nations. The boy said, "Wampum shall bring and bind peace and it shall take the place of blood." ◭

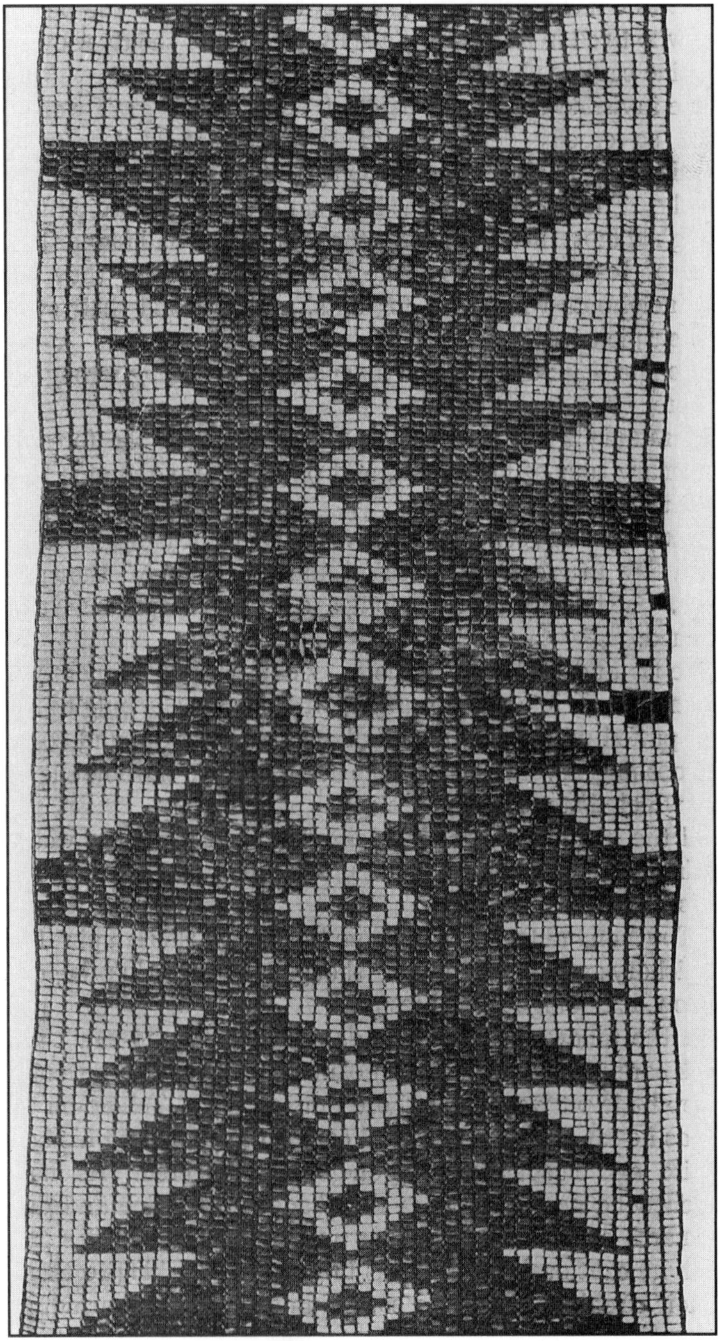

A section of an important Iroquois wampum belt known as the To-ta-da-ho. The series of white diamonds at the center of the belt symbolizes the binding together of the Five Nations into the Iroquois Confederacy.

CHAPTER 3

One Heart, One Mind, One Law

As a people, the Mohawks stressed friendliness, generosity, and consideration of others. These principles were obvious in the way they shared their food or goods with others, the way they comforted each other in times of crisis, and their belief that people should respect all others' rights. Their highest cultural value was unity, or many acting as one, which became the basis for the system of government the Mohawks helped create, which enabled the separate Iroquois nations to unite. Their motto was One Heart, One Mind, One Law.

This had not always been the case. The Iroquoian nations fought often with each other. In the 1300s or 1400s, two chiefs who had been adopted from other tribes by the Mohawks were determined to stop the fighting. Hiawatha (hi-ya-WA-ta) and Deganawida (de-ga-na-WEE-da) wanted to create a confederacy that would unite all five nations in a great peace. The confederacy would be made up of the Mohawks, the Oneidas, the Onondagas, the Cayugas, and the Senecas.

The story of Deganawida, the Peacemaker, has been handed down from generation to generation among the Mohawks. His mother had a dream that her son would be a messenger of the Creator and that he would bring peace to the people on earth. When Deganawida became a man, he knew that his purpose in life was to be a peacemaker, and he set off to create peace among warring nations. He met some evil people along the way and helped them to change. He finally reached the village of the Mohawk nation. When Deganawida gave the Mohawks his message of peace, they said that before they could believe him they must put him to a test.

He climbed to the top of a tree next to a waterfall. The warriors cut down the tree, and Deganawida fell over the cliff into the water and was carried over the falls. They thought he was dead. The next day some children came across a man sitting next to his fire. It was the Peacemaker, and the Mohawks were now ready to accept his message.

In the meantime, a man named Hiawatha, a member of the Onondaga nation, was trying to teach his people about peace and unity, but no one seemed to be interested. Then a great dreamer dreamed that Hiawatha would meet a traveling man and go with him to Mohawk territory. Someone began to use witchcraft against Hiawatha in order to force him to follow his dream: all of his seven daughters died one by one of mysterious causes. Hiawatha's grief was so great that he had to leave.

Finally, at a Mohawk village, Deganawida and Hiawatha met. The Peacemaker asked Hiawatha if he had plenty of shells. Hiawatha had gathered many shells from the bottom of a lake. With 15 strings of wampum, the Peacemaker helped to clear Hiawatha's mind of grief. The two men then set out together to create peace among the Iroquois nations.

Deganawida traveled to the various nations to ask for their consent to form the

f. 15.   *p. 12.*

Cet Jcy un
depute du bourg de gannachiou-
avé pourAlles inuites au jeu les
Messieurs de gandaougoaga.
Jls tiennent que le ser pontast
ledieu du feu, Jls linuoquent
le tenant en main en danfant
et chantant.

An 18th-century French drawing of a tattooed Mohawk man. The turtle on the man's thigh probably indicates that the man was a member of the Turtle clan.

confederacy. The leader of the Onondaga, Thadodaho (ta-do-DA-ho), at first said no, but once he met Deganawida, he agreed, but he wanted his nation to be "first among equals." The other Iroquois peoples agreed, and the world's first federal-style government was born. (Under a federal government, a number of individual entities—such as the 50 United States—agree to join together by surrendering some of their powers to a central government.) Each Iroquois nation remained independent, but the Five Nations agreed to decide important issues together in a Grand Council.

The symbol of the Iroquois Confederacy was a great longhouse that stretched from east to west. Because the Onondaga nation was in the center of Iroquois territory, councils were always held there, and the Onondagas were given the privilege of announcing council meetings. It was their duty to keep the council fire burning, and in the council longhouse the Onondagas therefore became the "fire keepers." The Mohawks were called the Keepers of the Eastern Door because they were located in the easternmost part of the Iroquois nation. The Senecas were the Keepers of the Western Door because they lived in the westernmost part of the Iroquois nation.

Originally, there were 50 hereditary chiefs among the Iroquois Confederacy, most of them with a title or name that was passed on to another man of the same clan after the chief's death. Two of the titles were never passed on—those belonging to Deganawida and Hiawatha. The chiefs were chosen by elder women of their clan and were expected to be intelligent, generous, and of good judgment. Meetings were held at least once a year, but the chiefs could meet whenever they felt the need. There were war chiefs as well as peace chiefs. The job of the war chiefs was to discuss and plan military expeditions. Though they could speak at confederacy meetings, they could not participate in decision making.

The confederacy council could take no action unless everyone was in agreement. The Onondagas always announced the topic of discussion and passed it on to the Mohawks for their thoughts, who in turn passed it on to the Seneca chiefs. The Senecas passed it back to the Mohawks, who announced the combined decision of the Mohawks and the Senecas. (The Mohawks, the Senecas, and the Onondagas made up one moiety of the Five Nations of the Iroquois, while the Cayugas and the Oneidas made up the other. The representatives of the two moieties always sat on opposite sides of the council fire.) Next, the Oneidas and the Cayugas discussed the matter. They declared their decision to a Mohawk chief, who announced the results to the Onondagas. If the Onondagas agreed, the decision was unanimous. If even one person disagreed, the matter was set aside, and the council fire was covered up with ashes. The covering of the fire symbolized the inability of the chiefs to agree, or to "roll their words into one bundle," as the Iroquois put it. At the end of a session, the actions of the council were "read into" the belts of wampum.

The form of government created by Deganawida and Hiawatha was well ahead of its time, and it enabled the Iroquois Confederacy to become one of the most powerful Indian nations in North America. Founding Father Benjamin Franklin greatly admired the Iroquois Confederacy, and he had it in mind when he first started thinking about how the 13 American colonies could unite as an independent nation. ▲

CHAPTER **4**

Broken Dreams

Large numbers of Europeans began to settle in North America in the 1600s. The Mohawks had heard about Europeans long before they met white men face-to-face. News about the new types of tools, clothing, and weapons that European traders offered in exchange for beaver furs spread quickly along the various Native American trading networks. Beaver hats and collars were extremely popular in Holland, France, and Great Britain, and beaver could be obtained only in North America. The Indians, on the other hand, wanted the metal objects and

woolen cloth brought to North America by the Europeans.

Once they began trading with the newcomers, the Mohawks quickly came to prefer the metal tools and utensils brought by the Europeans over their own handicrafts. In a short time, they stopped practicing such traditional skills as pottery making and toolmaking. Soon, the Mohawks were almost totally

The French explorer Samuel de Champlain made this illustration of his victorious encounter with the Mohawks at Lake Champlain in 1609.

dependent on the Europeans for various goods and necessities, and Mohawk men spent more and more time trapping beavers.

The fur trade became the single most important part of the Mohawk economy. Before the fur trade became so important to them, the Mohawks had been careful to hunt only as many animals as they needed for food and clothing, but now the Mohawks had to kill more and more beavers in order to obtain the goods they needed. Soon, all the beavers in the lands controlled by the Mohawks were gone, and the Mohawks resorted to fighting with other Indian peoples in order to obtain beaver pelts. Baron Louis de Lahontan, a French explorer who visited Mohawk territory in the late 1600s, thought that the Mohawks had little choice but to go to war. Without beaver pelts, Lahontan wrote, the Mohawks "would be starved to death, or at least obliged to leave their country."

Fighting over the fur trade began soon after Europeans started settling near Mohawk territory. The first major conflict involving the Mohawks and Europeans took place in 1609, when a group of Mohawk warriors were attacked at Lake Champlain by a group of Huron Indians, Algonkian Indians, and French soldiers led by the famous French explorer Samuel de Champlain. (Lake Champlain is at the northernmost extent of the border between the present-day states of New York and Vermont.) The battle marked the Mohawks' first experience with another item that Europeans brought to North America—guns. Although the Mohawks greatly outnumbered their enemy, the guns of the French force helped it to win the battle easily. The next year, the Mohawks were again easily defeated by the French and their Indian allies in a battle near the Richelieu River in Canada. This time, more than 100 Mohawk men were killed by French guns.

Meanwhile, the European population near Iroquois territory was steadily growing. More and more French were settling along the St. Lawrence River in Canada, and in 1615 the Dutch built Fort Orange, a trading post, along the Hudson River on the site of what is now the city of Albany, New York. Fort Orange was located between the territories of the Mohawks and the Mahican Indians. Both of these Indian peoples wanted to control the fur trade with the Dutch; both wanted to be the only ones to supply the Dutch with beaver pelts.

The Mohawks won the war with the Mahicans, and the Dutch introduced them to additional trade items. The Mohawks especially liked brass kettles, iron hunting tools, duffel cloth, biscuits, and flour. The Dutch also traded in wampum, which they obtained from Indians living on Long Island. The warfare between Indian peoples for control of the fur trade became more intense. The Mohawks soon proved themselves to be the fiercest warriors, especially once they began obtaining guns from the Dutch in the 1640s.

In a short time, the Mohawks controlled the most important waterways for the fur trade—the Hudson, St. Lawrence, and Richelieu rivers. They raided westward to the Great Lakes, northward into Canada, and eastward into New England. The Mohawks forced the Indian peoples living in those regions to supply them with beaver pelts for trade with the Europeans. In some cases, the Mohawks acted as middlemen in trade between the Indians and the Europeans. Often, Mohawk warriors would ambush the fleets of canoes sent by other Indian tribes to Fort Orange or to Montreal or Quebec in Canada. The Mohawks even drove several tribes, including the Huron and the Erie, from their homelands.

The Mohawks were as skilled at diplomacy as they were at warfare. They were superb traders and negotiators, and they used the competition between the different European groups—the French, the English, and the Dutch—for control of the northern part of

North America to their own advantage. They traded with the British, who were competing with the Dutch for control of the fur trade around Fort Orange, and they traded with the Dutch as well. Although the French had been their enemy since the time of the battle at Lake Champlain, the Mohawks also traded with them when it was to their advantage to do so. Though the Mohawks preferred British trade goods, which were very well made, they kept on trading with the French in order to force the British traders to keep their prices low.

All the while, the number of Europeans who wanted to settle in Mohawk territory continued to grow. The Dutch settlers were generally fair in purchasing land from the Mohawks, but they were never very numerous, and they were quickly outnumbered by the British. The British were less fair to the Mohawks and used a variety of ways to trick the Indians out of their land. One of the most common methods was to convince the Mohawks to sign papers that they could not read or understand. The Mohawks would be told that they had agreed to one thing, only to learn later that they had signed papers that committed them to something very different.

Still, the Mohawks tended to support the British militarily against the French, primarily because they wished to maintain good trade relations. The British, however, were often untrustworthy allies. In the 1660s, a huge French and Indian force marched against the Mohawks' villages, burned their houses, and torched their cornfields, and the British did nothing to help. Several years later, a smaller French army again attacked the Mohawks, and the British again did nothing.

Although the British took their land and betrayed their trust, the Mohawks had little choice but to maintain their alliance with them. By the end of the 1600s, the British in New York had come to outnumber the Iroquois. While the number of British colonists steadily increased, the Iroquois population dwindled. Even more than warfare, disease reduced the Indian population. The European settlers brought with them to North America all kinds of diseases—smallpox, measles, influenza—for which the Indians had no immunity, and the Iroquois suffered terribly. Epidemics claimed the lives of many of the Mohawk people.

Though the Iroquois remained one of the most powerful Indian nations, they recognized that they were no longer a match for the English. In 1684, an Iroquois chief told a British army officer at Albany, "You are a mighty leader and we are but a small people.

When the English first came to New York, Virginia, and Maryland, they were but a small people and we a large nation. We found that they were a good people and gave them land and dealt civilly with them. Now that you are grown numerous and we decreased, you must protect us."

But it was religion, not warfare, that posed the greatest threat to the One Heart, One Mind, One Law of the Mohawks. A French Catholic priest, Isaac Jogues, in 1642 became the first missionary to reach the Iroquois. He would be followed by many more Catholic clergymen from France, all of them eager to convert the Mohawks to Christianity.

The missionaries, who were called Black Robes by the Indians, were not immediately successful. Jogues hoped to establish a mission in Mohawk territory, but the Indians were not very interested in his teachings, and he soon left. When he did, he accidentally left behind a black box in which he had stored his things. Soon after he departed, large numbers of Mohawks began to get sick and die. For the next four years, the Mohawk villages were devastated by disease. The Mohawks concluded that Father Jogues had bewitched the black box and that the sermons he had spoken to them contained evil charms and spells. When he returned to the Mohawks in 1646, they killed him.

continued on page 49

BEADWORK AND BASKETRY

Crafts remain an important part of Mohawk Indian life. By creating beadwork and baskets just as their ancestors did, the Mohawks help keep their customs alive.

Long ago, the Mohawks used purple and white beads to make wampum belts. After they began obtaining glass beads through trade with Europeans, the Mohawks used beadwork for decoration on clothing and other objects.

Basketry is another meaningful form of Mohawk art. It includes tasks performed by both men and women. Those Mohawks living on the Akwesasne Reservation in New York state especially treasure this craft. The men cut black ash trees, pound the trunks, and break the wood into strips. Women cut and smooth these strips to make thin splints. The women also collect and dry wild sweet grass, which they weave into the splints. The result of all this hard work is a strong, textured, and sweet–smelling basket.

Traditionally, the Mohawks made large, simple baskets, which they used to store food. Today, some of their baskets are small and fancy and are used as containers, and others are made to be small sculptures.

A rope necklace made from glass beads. Louise McComber, Wolf Clan, Kahnawake Reserve.

Muriel Nicholas, a member of the Bear Clan, beading at her home on the Oka Reserve.

A leather collar adorned with a beaded image of an eagle. Rita Phillips, Wolf Clan, Kahnawake Reserve.

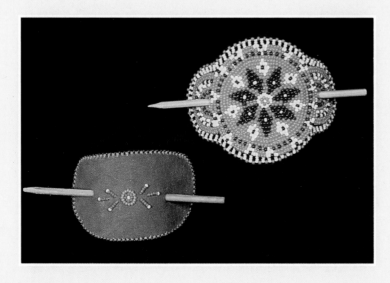

Barrettes made from glass beads and leather. Agnes Decaire, Kahnawake Reserve.

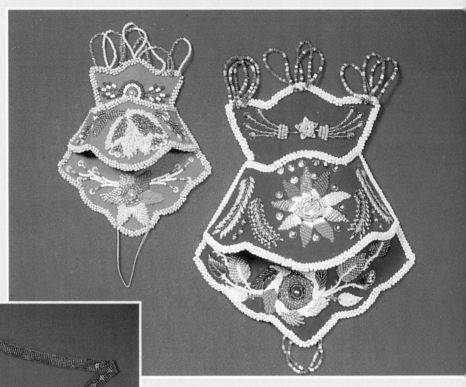

Two cloth whisk-broom holders decorated with floral beadwork designs. Mary Scott Jacobs, Wolf Clan, Kahnawake Reserve.

A glass bead medallion that was woven on a loom. Adeline Etienne, Bear Clan, Oka Reserve.

44

A bandolier bag made from cloth. The beaded design represents the Celestial Tree, which is described in the Mohawk's creation story. David Maracle, Turtle Clan, Tyendinega Reserve.

Mary Adams, a member of the Wolf Clan and resident of the Akwe-sasne Reservation, has handcrafted baskets for more than 50 years.

Adams presented this basket to Pope John Paul II in 1980 when 17th-century Mohawk religious figure Kateli Tekakwitha was beatified by the Roman Catholic church.

A lidded basket crafted to commemorate the Strawberry Festival held every June at Akwesasne. Christie Arquette, Turtle Clan, Akwesasne Reservation.

A fancy basket with cover. Cecelia Cree, Wolf Clan, Akwesasne Reservation.

A multicolor fancy basket woven by Mary Adams.

continued from page 40

Though the Indians were right that Father Jogues had brought disease to them, witchcraft was not the cause. Like other Europeans, the French priest had brought more than trade goods, a desire for land, or a new religion with him. He carried germs for which the Indians had no immunity. Throughout North America, missionaries unintentionally spread deadly diseases among Native Americans in this way.

The Black Robes came again to the Mohawks in 1656. Though the missionaries did not intend to destroy the Mohawk people, their effect was devastating because they did set out to eliminate many of the beliefs and customs that had held the Mohawks together for hundreds of years. For example, some French priests believed that the way the Mohawks tried to understand and fulfill their dreams was a sign of devil worship, and they made it their goal to rid the Mohawks of such beliefs. They also tried to change the indulgent way the Mohawks raised their children. They tried to teach the Mohawks that children must be obedient and should be punished if they misbehaved. The priests also did not believe that married couples should be able to divorce. A Mohawk marriage usually lasted until the death of one partner, but if a wife and husband became unhappy with one another they were free to divorce and seek new mates. The mothers of the couple would step in first, however, and try to help settle any arguments. The priests worked to change this custom.

Although the Mohawks were not greatly interested in converting to Christianity, they accepted the missionaries because they thought that by doing so they could improve their relations with the French, which might lead to increased trade. The priests were impressed with the military skills of the Mohawks and with the generosity of their society, in which no one was allowed to go hungry or be poor. They were, however, often frustrated with the Mohawks' refusal to embrace Christianity or to accept an allegiance with the French against the British, and they went so far as to advise the government of France to step up attacks against them. They believed that if the Mohawks were defeated, the other four Iroquois nations would agree to a treaty with France.

The French never defeated the Mohawks militarily, but the missionaries won a great victory when they succeeded in convincing some of the Mohawks to convert to Catholicism. In 1667, the priests talked the converts into leaving their land and people behind and moving to missions near Montreal, where, they said, the Catholic Mohawks would be safe near French forts. Because of their new religion, the converts were distrusted by their families and neighbors. Their new settlement in Canada was called Kahnawake (gah-na-WA-ge), after their former village in New York. Nine years later, another group of Catholic Mohawks formed a new settlement in Canada, also near Montreal. The new village was called Kanesatake (ga-ne-sa-DA-ge). In a short time the Canadian Mohawks adopted European ways and values, which made them seem very strange to the New York Mohawks.

The Mohawks in New York were greatly upset over this division in their formerly close-knit society. This was the first time there had been a split in Mohawk unity. They worried that the French would soon talk the

The longhouses of the Mohawk settlement of Kahwanake. The settlement was founded near Montreal, Canada, in 1667 by Mohawks who had converted to Catholicism.

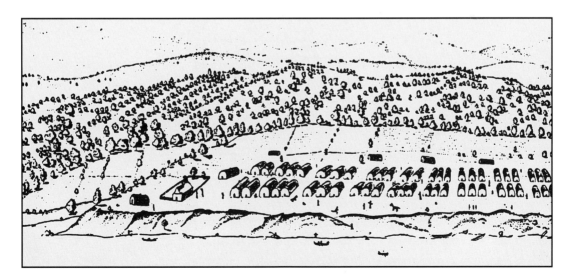

Christian Mohawks into fighting their own people. Although the Indians at Kahnawake and Kanesatake tried to remain neutral in the Iroquois-French conflicts, they often found themselves fighting for France or trying to convince the New York Mohawks to side with the French in their battles against the British.

Queen Anne's War pitted the soldiers of Great Britain and France against one another in North America between 1702 and 1713, and it caused the greatest rift to that point between the New York Mohawks and the Canadian Mohawks. As in the past, the Mohawks were pressured to take sides. The Iroquois, including the New York Mohawks, fought on the side of the English, and the Catholic Mohawks in Canada fought for the French.

At this point, the British tried to use some of the same methods the French had used to secure the loyalty of the Mohawks and the other Iroquois. They sent missionaries to convert the Mohawks to Christianity, and they built a fort for the protection of the Mohawks. But the New York Mohawks were not particularly interested in becoming Christians, and the British continued to cheat the Mohawks out of huge sections of their homeland. Each year, more settlers came to Iroquois country. The Mohawks petitioned

The Mohawk chief Brant was one of several Mohawk leaders who were invited to England to speak with the queen during Queen Anne's War.

the king of England, George III, for help, but nothing was done to prevent illegal sales of Iroquois land. The Indians did not understand European methods of measuring land, and they could not read land deeds. They were thus cheated out of hundreds and even thousands of acres.

During this time a sixth nation joined the Iroquois Confederacy. The Tuscaroras were an Iroquoian people who had been living in Virginia at the time of the arrival of Europeans in North America. When the English began taking over their territories, the Tuscaroras asked the Iroquois in the north for protection and a place of safety. They were admitted to the confederacy in 1722.

Over the next several decades, Protestant missionaries from Great Britain continued their efforts to convert the Mohawks to Christianity, with greater success. They opened schools where religion was taught at two Mohawk villages, and they urged the Mohawks to form closer ties with the British. But the disputes over land ownership continued, and in 1753 a Mohawk chief named Hendrick announced that the "chain of friendship" between his people and the British was now broken. Finally, the Mohawks announced that the chain of friendship between all the Iroquois nations and Great Britain was broken. The British promised that they would treat the Mohawks more fairly, and when the French and Indian War began in 1756, the Mohawks once again promised to support their old allies.

The French and Indian War, which lasted seven years, was the final battle between the

British and the French for control of eastern North America. The British won, in large part because of the help of the Mohawks, who suffered many casualties. The Mohawks hoped to be rewarded for their service with years of peace on the small amount of land they still owned, but they were soon caught in the middle of a new fight. ▲

The great Mohawk chief and orator Joseph Brant tried to persuade the Iroquois Confederacy to side with the British during the American Revolution.

CHAPTER 5

The Mohawks and the American Revolution

By the 1770s, many of the inhabitants of the 13 colonies believed that the colonies should declare their independence. They resented being made to pay taxes to the British crown when they were not represented in Parliament. (Parliament was the legislative body for Great Britain, just as the Congress is the legislative body for the United States.)

The colonists were also angered by Britain's attempt to restrict their settlement to lands east of the Appalachian Mountains and south of the Ohio River. These disagreements led ultimately to the American Revolution, which began on April 19, 1775, with a skirmish between British redcoats and colonial minutemen at the villages of Lexington and Concord in Massachusetts. On July 4, 1776, the 13 colonies officially proclaimed their independence from Great Britain.

The rebellious colonists were aware that the Iroquois were loyal to the British, and they knew that the Mohawks could make a huge difference in the outcome of the war, as they had in the French and Indian War. In 1775, therefore, some leaders of the American rebels invited some of the Iroquois leaders to Albany for a meeting. The Americans offered to give them supplies, especially warm clothing, if they would promise to remain neutral in the quarrel between the colonists and England. The Iroquois agreed, but only on the condition that the colonists promise to resolve some land disputes that had taken place.

The British were still determined to have the help of their old allies. They promised the Iroquois that whatever property they lost during the war would be restored to them by the king of England afterward. The British also knew that the best way to gain the loyalty of the Iroquois was to become their only supplier of European goods, which they achieved by defeating an American force, led by George Washington, that was in New York City. That victory cut off the supply of goods the Americans had intended for the Iroquois, for the goods arrived in New York Harbor aboard ships from Europe.

British leaders secured further Iroquois support by courting important Indian leaders, such as the Mohawk chief Joseph Brant, who traveled to England to speak with King George and other government leaders about fighting for Britain. Upon his return, Brant spoke to a council meeting of the Iroquois Confederacy in support of Great Britain in its fight with the colonists. The Mohawks, the Senecas, and the Cayugas agreed with his arguments, while the Oneidas and the Tuscaroras favored the American rebels. The Onondagas were divided among themselves.

Unable to reach an agreement, the confederacy leaders sadly covered up the council fire at the central Onondaga village, and the confederacy officially remained neutral. The results of the council pleased no one, and individual Mohawks made their own decisions about which side to support. The principle of unity—One Heart, One Mind, One Law—had been violated, and the Iroquois Confederacy, which had stressed strength through unity, would never be as strong again.

Joseph Brant and his many followers continued to support the British, who supplied the Mohawks with tools, clothing, and weapons. Many Mohawks felt that although they did not fully trust the British, they had no choice but to support them, especially once the colonial legislature of New York claimed all Indian land within the state and offered 600 acres of it to anyone who joined the rebel forces. To the Mohawks, such actions seemed to prove that the British were right in saying that an American victory would mean the end of Indian control over their land. Though most of the Mohawks remained neutral, American rebels burned their crops, stole their livestock, and attacked them as acts of revenge against the Iroquois warriors who were fighting with the British.

The Americans won the war, but American independence meant less freedom for the Mohawks. Britain relinquished all land claims in North America east of the Mississippi and south of Canada. This territory included the land that the Mohawks regarded as their own.

This drawing of the Mohawk reserve of Akwesasne was done in the 1850s. Akwesasne, which straddles the New York–Canada border, is also known as St. Regis.

The new government of the United States was not sympathetic when the Mohawks argued that the British had no right to surrender their land, especially since so many Iroquois had fought against American independence. The Americans made no effort to keep settlers out of Iroquois territory, and by the end

of the 1780s most of the Mohawks had moved to Canada. There, most of them settled in the five Mohawk villages that had been established there over the preceding years: Kahnawake, Kanesatake, Akwesasne (ah-gwe-SAS-ne), Tyendinega (ti-yen-di-NE-ga), and Six Nations, where peoples of all the Iroquois nations settled and the confederacy fire was reestablished.

In Canada in the years following the American Revolution, the Mohawks tried to adapt to new lives in a new society. They continued to hunt, fish, and farm, and they began to raise pigs, poultry, and horses. Newcomers from other Indian groups came to their land and were accepted. As the fur trade died out, Mohawk men became loggers, trappers, and canoeists. Some traveled west across Canada and married into other Indian communities. In time the Canadian government set aside the Mohawks' land as protected enclaves called *reserves*. (A reserve is the same thing as a reservation in the United States.)

Other policies of the Canadian government were more destructive to the Mohawks. At various periods throughout the 1800s, the government created policies designed to destroy the traditional Mohawk system of owning their land in common. Instead, the

Mohawk men at work on a bridge in the late 1800s. By that time, many Mohawks had come to rely on wage work rather than hunting, trapping, or farming for their living.

government divided Mohawk reserves into small plots, called allotments, that were to be owned by individuals. Such policies were a further blow to the Mohawks' concept of unity, and they greatly diminished the role of Mohawk women in their community. At Six Nations, the Canadian government also required that the Mohawks be governed by elected representatives rather than by hereditary chiefs, and women were not allowed to vote.

Despite the many hardships of their life on the reserves in the 1800s, the Mohawks managed to maintain many of the traditions that had enabled them to survive as a people for so long. They also developed new traditions that helped them as well. Although missionaries controlled education on the reserves for many years, by the end of the 1800s the Mohawks had established 13 schools of their own. The Mohawks' schools enabled them to pass on their traditions to their children and therefore ensure that their beliefs would endure.

During this time, many Mohawks also became believers in a new religion, called the Handsome Lake Religion or the Longhouse Religion. Handsome Lake was a Seneca man who lived in the early 1800s. In a dream, he received a vision that he was to preach a new message to the Iroquois. Handsome Lake's message, which he called the *Good Word*, stressed the traditional Iroquois values of generosity, cooperation, and kindness. Although he also advocated that the Iroquois adopt some Canadian and American practices, the religion he founded did much to help the Mohawks maintain pride in themselves, their past, and their culture. ⏶

WHY OUR CHILDREN SHOULD KNOW THEIR LANGUAGE AND HAVE INDIAN NAMES

Our children must have a name in their native language so the Creator will know them when they pass from this world to the next. All of the Ceremonies must be done in our language as the creator taught us. When no person of our nation speaks our language we will no longer exist as

ONKWEHONWE.

This poster was designed to show Mohawk children the importance of learning their native language.

CHAPTER 6

The Mohawks in the 20th Century

In the 20th century, the Mohawks have once again shown their ability to adapt to changing circumstances. Today, most Mohawks work for wages. They are employed in businesses and factories in towns and cities. Some men work as miners, carpenters, mechanics, factory hands, or builders. Others work in automobile factories in Buffalo, New York, and Oakville, Ontario. Women are employed as nurses, teachers, factory workers, or service employees.

Most Akwesasne and Kahnawake men have spent some part of their lives employed in high-steel construction. They work in places such as Rochester, Boston, New York City, Buffalo, and Syracuse, building bridges and skyscrapers. It is not uncommon for them to live in city apartments during the week and return to their reserves on the weekend. Groups of men live, work, and travel together.

Some Mohawks live and work in their communities. At the three largest reserves—Six Nations, Kahnawake, and Akwesasne—jobs are available in band offices, schools, restaurants, stores, and gas stations. On smaller reserves, cranberry farms produce 10 to 25 percent of Canada's supply of this fruit. Still, more people work off the reserve than on.

The conflict over elected versus hereditary leaders on the Six Nations reserve continues. Because only about one-third of the Mohawks there vote, some people have argued that the elective system does not work especially well. Some people believe that so few Mohawks vote because they do not really care who their leaders are, but others believe that the voter turnout is so low because most Mohawks do not like the elective system and would prefer to have hereditary chiefs as their leaders. In 1959, the hereditary chiefs tried to regain their leadership positions at Six Nations by taking over the council offices. They stayed one week before the Royal Canadian Mounted Police forced them to leave. At Kahnawake and Akwesasne, hereditary chiefs continue to be respected members of the community even though they do not hold elective office.

Land continues to be a major issue for the Mohawks. Instead of fighting with guns, the Mohawks have had to learn how to fight for their land in the political and legal system. In the 1950s, the governments of Canada and the United States took more land from the Kahnawake Mohawks in order to build the St. Lawrence Seaway, a series of locks, dams, and canals along the St. Lawrence River that would connect the Atlantic Ocean and the Great Lakes. They offered money to the Indians for their land, but the Mohawks refused their offer. The U.S. and Canadian governments then simply took the land. The Mohawks took their case to the United Nations, which was sympathetic but did not help.

On other matters concerning their right to self-determination, the Mohawks have been more successful. In 1969, for example, they blockaded a bridge that spans the St. Lawrence River and connects the American and Canadian sides of Akwesasne. (Akwesasne is also known as the St. Regis Reserve or the St. Regis Reservation, and it occupies territory on both sides of the U.S.–Canada border.) The Mohawks were angry because the Canadian government had established a customs station and toll booth at the bridge and were subjecting the Indians to customs inspections and forcing them to pay tolls each time they crossed. The Indians believed that according to a 1794 treaty, they had the right to cross the border whenever they pleased. After years of Mohawk opposition and protests, they were finally granted the right to free passage in the 1980s.

The most important issue for the Mohawks continues to be self-determination—the right to govern their own nation and control their own destiny. The Mohawks believe that the right to self-determination, or sovereignty, has been granted to them in many treaties over the years, but local and national governments in the United States and Canada have often been reluctant to recognize this right.

The Mohawks expressed their belief on this matter in 1970, in the course of a dispute over land with New York State. "We are not citizens of state or nation," Mohawk leaders said at that time. "We have our own nation—the Six Nations. You have no right to legislate for us or us for you." In l984, officials in Quebec signed an agreement with the Kah-

In recent years, the Mohawks have been more assertive about claiming their right to self-determination. In the mid-1970s, armed Mohawk men occupied a tract of land in upstate New York for three years. They called the site Ganienkeh (Ga-NYEN-ge) and claimed it was just a small part of a much larger territory that rightfully belonged to the Mohawk nation.

nawake Council to construct a hospital on the reserve. It was the first time the Canadian government had recognized the government of an Indian band as its equal.

Even though the reserves are scattered across Canada and New York State, there is more unity among the Mohawks than people might at first believe. When a land dispute was going on at Kanesatake and the Mo-

hawks blockaded a road leading to the area in question, Indian groups throughout Canada began erecting blockades in their territories to show their support.

In 1970, serious problems were found on the reserves in the areas of education, health, and housing. Federal monies were given to the reserves to promote bilingual and bicultural education. (Bilingual and bicultural education means that Mohawk children would learn their own language as well as English, and learn about their own culture and history as well as about the culture and history of the rest of Canadian society.) Several groups have published books to help teach children the Mohawk language. A poster supporting bilingual education for the Mohawks explained why it was important for Mohawk children to know their own language and have Indian names. "Our children must have a name in their native language so the Creator will know them when they pass from this world to the next," the poster read. "When no person of our nation speaks our language we will no longer exist as Onkwehonwe." *Onkwehonwe* (on-gwe-HON-we) is the Mohawk word for Native American. It means "real people."

In 1990, a dispute on the Akwesasne reserve over casino gambling grew violent, and police from New York and Canada oc-

Mohawk children in school at Akwesasne. In recent decades the Mohawks have made a great effort to ensure that their children's education includes lessons in their traditional heritage and culture.

cupied the reserve for several weeks. The disagreement is between the hereditary chiefs and their followers, who do not feel that gambling fits into the traditional Mohawk way of life, and the elected leaders and their followers, who believe that the huge amounts of money that could be made on the reserve from casino gambling could be used to create jobs, provide for education, and generally improve the Indians' standard of living. The Mohawk Council of Chiefs appealed to the U.S. government for help in settling the issue, but the dispute still has not been resolved. In October 1990, however, a committee of the New York State Assembly

The 1978 lacrosse team of the Akwesasne reserve. Lacrosse is just one of the many cultural traditions that the Mohawks have preserved in the modern age.

suggested that the Mohawks be able to choose whatever form of government the community wants.

The Mohawks are one of the many Indian societies that have managed to survive wars waged against them, forced migration to other lands, and the pressure to adapt to other peoples' ways of life. Though it is unlikely that they will be able to re-create a government like the original Iroquois Confederacy—to be once again of One Heart, One Mind, One Law—the more than 40,000 Mohawks who live today on the various reserves remain determined to protect their rights and live the way they choose. They still have every reason to feel pride in being the People of the Place of Flint, the Keepers of the Eastern Door. ▲

CHRONOLOGY

1700–1200 B.C.	Iroquois migrate to northeastern New York
A.D. 200	Middle Woodland period of the Iroquois
A.D. 1000–1300	The Mohawks form their own nation
ca. 1300 or 1400	The Mohawks form the Iroquois Confederacy with the Senecas, the Onondagas, the Oneidas, and the Cayugas
1609	The Mohawks are defeated in battle by French and Indian forces led by Samuel de Champlain
1642	The Mohawks have their first encounter with a missionary, the French priest Isaac Jogues
1660s	The Mohawks are attacked by 1,200 French troops and their 600 Indian allies; settlers take an increasing amount of Mohawk land; converted Mohawks leave their homeland for a Catholic mission in Canada
1722	A sixth Indian Nation, the Tuscaroras, joins Iroquois Confederacy
1756–63	The Mohawks help the British to victory in the French and Indian War
1770s	Confederacy leaders cannot agree on which side to support in the American Revolution
1780s	Many Mohawks leave New York for Canada
1924	Canadian government forces the Mohawks to elect leaders
1984	Canadian government recognizes the Mohawks as a sovereign equal
1990	A committee of the New York State Assembly suggests the Mohawks be allowed to choose whatever form of government the community wants

GLOSSARY

confederacy   a union of tribes or nations that functions as one unit; see Five Nations

Five Nations   the confederacy of the five Iroquois tribes (the Mohawks, the Senecas, the Oneidas, the Cayugas, and the Onondagas); when the Tuscaroras joined the confederacy it became the Six Nations

Good Word   a religion created by a Seneca named Handsome Lake, who stressed traditional Iroquois values such as generosity, cooperation, and kindness

Kanienkehaka   the name the Mohawks call themselves in their own language, meaning the People of the Place of Flint

longhouse   a large, bark-covered dwelling that housed several Mohawk families

Midwinter   a major Mohawk religious ceremony that marked the end of one year and the beginning of the next.

moiety   a basic division of the Mohawk nation, a grouping of clans

Onkwehonwe   the Mohawk word for Native American, named for the first "red man" created by Teharonhiawako

reserve   the Canadian term for reservation; land set aside by the government for use by a specific group of Indians

Teharonhiawako   in the Mohawk creation story, the name of the man who created the four races—yellow, white, black, and red

INDEX

ABOUT THE AUTHOR

JANET HUBBARD-BROWN has a B.A. in Modern Humanities from New York University and is the author of three non-fiction books for children. She lives with her husband and two children in Fayston, Vermont, where she is working on a children's book about Lizzie Borden.

PICTURE CREDITS